My Voice Cannot Be Bombed

Published by *Iskra Books* © 2025
Copyright retained by the author *Yahya Al Hamarna* © 2025

10 9 8 7 6 5 4 3 2 1

All rights reserved.
The moral rights of the author have been asserted.

RED POETRY COLLECTION

ISKRA BOOKS
WWW.ISKRABOOKS.ORG
US | ENGLAND | IRELAND

Iskra Books is an independent scholarly publisher—publishing original works of revolutionary theory, history, education, and art, as well as edited collections, new translations, and critical republications of older works.

ISBN-13: 978-1-0881-1635-7 (SOFTCOVER)

British Library Cataloguing in Publication Data
A catalogue record for this book is available from the British Library.

Library of Congress Cataloging-in-Publication Data
A catalog record for this book is available from the Library of Congress

Typesetting by RÓISÍN DUBH and BEN STAHNKE
Cover Art by BEN STAHNKE
Final Page Artwork by AREEJ KAOUD © 2023

My Voice Cannot Be Bombed

Yahya Al Hamarna

**An Iskra
Red Poetry Book**

Above: The author, Yahya Al Hamarna—taken in Al Mawasi, Gaza, Palestine, 8th December, 2024.

When I tell my dear friend
the pen
that we will write,
especially about Palestine,
it immediately tells me,
"Let's write together.
We are stronger than the
cowardly occupation."

How beautiful it is to write
about our heart and our
beloved Palestine.

Palestine makes us stronger,
my friend.

Writing is not just letters on paper; it is an act of survival, a voice of resistance, and a promise for tomorrow.

It is my commitment to myself, to humanity, and to those who will come after us in this world stained with ash. In moments of bombardment, amidst displacement and hunger, I find in writing a space for deep understanding.

When words are spoken, they are chosen hastily, but when they are written, they pulsate with deep contemplation, a message that escapes loss.

My pen writes so that I don't forget, so that my memory isn't erased, so that I can survive.

Yahya Al Hamarna, a Palestinian refugee from under the rubble, writes so that he can live.

Writing is the last line of defense.

Contents

1 Daily Diary: When I Survive

5 And After a Long Wait, a Hug

7 Does Anyone See Us?

9 Pen

11 The Sound of the Birds

13 A Rescue Operation in Progress

16 I Pondered

18 A Paper Plane

20 In Just One Minute

24 Palestine Eid

26 Professor of the Art of Hope, Parts 1 & 2

DAILY DIARY
When I Survive

WHEN I SURVIVE

I won't rush to get to my university lectures

And I won't get angry if dinner is late

When I get back from my gym workout

I'll take a warm shower and think about making major decisions

I'll tell my mom I love you a thousand times

I'll make her hug me and kiss me

A smile and tenderness, so that her hug, and kiss on my face are with me everywhere like my imagination

I'll make popcorn and grape juice to watch a Robert De Niro movie in my little room.

I won't feel stressed during the week of final university exams

I will balance my studies with watching Real Madrid in the knockout stages of the Champions League, the Champions League nights, I will watch Vini and Valverde score goals

And I won't go home straight away, I will go for a walk in the park and smell the fresh air and the daffodils

When I get back home from the park

I will make my own food, cheese, tea, bread and olives

I will make a list of cities I want to visit, London, Rome, Brussels, Mallorca, Istanbul, Paris, Cardiff, a long list of cities because traveling will be a psychological relief and a vacation from this tiring life,

And Madrid to watch my favorite team there in the Spanish capital, I will watch the match with my friends and we will go to the cinema together

And I will read the weather news in the cities I want to visit to know how to choose my favorite weather

WHEN I SURVIVE

I will not stay up late, I will set an alarm early so I can wake up early, I want to sleep peacefully because for more than a whole year I have not slept well and I am tired of the insomnia that has eaten my body

And I will not go quickly in the morning to the grocery store, I will walk slowly to the park and smell the fresh air and drink coffee and read the newspaper

WHEN I START OVER

I will finish my first study in international relations and diplomacy,

And I will finally achieve success after stopping the genocide and completing my studies at Al-Azhar University so that the name of my university will be with me everywhere

I will make my graduation party with my birthday because I love to be born again with knowledge, we will celebrate together with my friends, I will be there at the Café Palestina in London and it will be a beautiful party finally,

I will read my articles and my graduation thesis, we will eat the delicious orange cake and smile a lot while taking souvenir photos, and after a beautiful day I will go home to make new success plans that I have drawn in my imagination.

When I survive

I will not have breakfast quickly, I will drink coffee and smell the air quietly with Fairuz's music, I will drink water with roses in the morning, as roses are my beautiful friend always with me on my desk in the room.

And I will not delay reading my mailbox in the morning, in the morning with the rise of a new sun a new hope is born with the sun

When I go to the city, I will take a big tour in the central library and smell the books, knowledge, culture, philosophy, history, politics, psychology, literature, poetry and many sciences,

I will make a list of books in law, politics, diplomacy and philosophy so that I can buy them from there, and I will write them with me in my daily notebook and I will live with these beautiful books, they will be my friend everywhere

I will read books, I will start to recover and I will heal with the pharmacy of books,

I will finally go to the garden with tea, cakes and sweets, smell the comfortable air and the sound of birds singing, and Yahya reading.

One day, one day, perhaps, soon, we will survive this genocide, let us dream again, let us see what will happen in the end, oh my friend.

24TH OCTOBER 2024

And After a Long Wait, a Hug

I will meet you soon, GAZA.
It's just a matter of days.
I will walk barefoot on the first step of your land;
I want my skin to touch and stick with you, my dear.
Your emptiness, and my longing for you, have filled the Earth,
the solar system, even the space and the Milky Way.
I love you so much, GAZA.
Your scent has a voice that reminds me of life—
Your sea, your air, the streets of your city,
The alleys of the camp, the university,
The breeze of the north, and the whispers at night.
I was so late to meet you,
But please, wait for me just one more week.
I will have an appointment with you—
I will hug you and kiss your soil,
And I will water your land with my tears.
I've tried so hard,
And now, with the approach of our meeting, I am born again.

My name is now among the survivors of genocide.
I will survive, and I will learn,
I will travel the world in your name.
I will raise your name everywhere: Free Palestine.
It feels like I have a permanent appointment with you.
The meeting is near,
The embrace is near,
The kissing of the earth is near.
Please, time—
Be swift this time.
I want my wound to finally heal-
By kissing your land, Gaza,
And sitting with you,
Talking about the journey of survival that has exhausted my body.

Gaza, our meeting is approaching.

19th January 2025

Does Anyone See Us?

Does anyone see us?

Does anyone see that we need sufficient light to look around us in the cold nights and eat a meal? Does anyone see us living in a tent with four leather walls and a dilapidated roof, unfit for living? Does anyone see us going out every day, carrying our phones, batteries, and radios to charge them at a solar-powered phone charging station? When the weather isn't sunny—like in winter—we can't charge our phones or even listen to the news on the radio. Does anyone see us walking several kilometers each day to find an internet signal, even a weak one? Does anyone see us trying to create simple, primitive self-education because the cowardly occupation has deprived innocent, defenseless civilians of the right to learn? Children and university students cannot study because the cowardly occupation has bombed schools and universities, destroying the educational system. Does anyone see us living without a health system because the depraved occupation has destroyed every aspect of healthcare in Gaza? Does anyone see us? Does anyone see us??!!

Finally, does anyone see us? We live on the same planet, in the same world—on the continent of Asia, near the Mediterranean Sea. We breathe the same air, and the Mediterranean Sea connects us to other countries and people. Yet we live without electricity, without water, without food, without medicine, and amidst bombing, displacement, killing, and massacres. Strangely, in this age of technology, social media, advanced media, the internet, artificial intelligence, and space exploration—no one sees us. Because when I ask, "Does anyone see us?" There is no answer.

27TH MARCH 2025

Pen

I walked slowly beside my grandfather, MUSTAFA,
on our way to Lebanon.
But we had misread the compass.
Instead of leading us there, it guided us
to beloved Gaza.
With each step, I carried hope in my heart—
hope that one day I would return
to my hometown, Zarnoqa in Palestine.

I believe that dreams do come true.
I learned that in school.

Suddenly, I was pulled from my imagination back into reality.
A cowardly soldier, with a rough voice
and a strange appearance, stopped us.
He asked, "Do you have any thoughts
of surrendering?"
I replied, "I don't know that word.
I haven't seen it in my dictionary."

Angered, he searched me
and then arrested me.

I was stunned. "Why?" I asked.
He said, "You're carrying a dangerous weapon."
I looked at him, confused. "What is it?"

"A pen," he replied.

All I had in my bag was a PEN.

2ND MAY 2025

The Sound of Birds

Good morning my adored homeland
It is 7AM in Jerusalem time, the capital of Palestine
Maybe I can say I am winning today
with the title of Active Man
I arranged the wood logs
and lit them up to make my coffee
and in my hand is Shakespeare's theatre work
The sky is clear and the sun is beautiful

Coffee
and a book
and calmness with the sound of birds chirping
The sound of children started coming out,
playing to forget the cruelty of the war a little
I face war and I make beautiful things
There are things stronger than the sound of bombings
which doesn't stop

I dream one day soon
to wake up,

me, and my neighbours, the kids
to the sound of birds that sing
without the sound of bombs
Without an evil and malicious bombing
Just the sound of birds
I don't want more,
than the sound of the birds

16th May 2025

A Rescue Operation in Progress

In my calm room,
I stand before my books—
half of which I lost
in the journey of displacement.
I stand alone.
And I write questions.
I have no power but this:
to write.

I am writing
a rescue operation in progress,
a rescue from facing sadness
Alone,
in silence.

A rescue of survival words
I whisper to myself every day:
When I survive, when I survive...
My heart urges me to dive into hope,

while my mind pleads, don't.
I'm trying to survive
in any way I can.

Sometimes, I can't—
I lose the desire
amid everything unfolding
before my innocent eyes.
The pain is larger than me.
I am writing
a rescue operation in progress:
families displaced,
homes destroyed,
mothers saying goodbye,
children weeping.
Everything here is painful.
The suffering swells each day
beneath this nightmare
that refuse to end.
I sit alone—there, alone—
to create a rescue operation,
to heal my grief,
to find strength again
to face the pains I witness daily.

And maybe, one day,
they will end.

I say, maybe
this rescue operation will succeed—

O Gaza,
may you survive
all this suffering.
O Gaza.

20ᵀᴴ May 2025

I Pondered

I think and feel
that one of the beautiful things
that happens to a human being
is to have enough POWER
to sit somewhere
far away from the sound of bombs and fear
that follow him
everywhere

Carrying with him a small notebook
and it is in his pocket always
He writes a lot of things
Past, present, and future
Hopes and fears and plans
Experiences and tears and moments
They remain preserved in memory
Writings that narrate
what we are living

Sometimes when I'm coming back from the beach near sundown
The moon starts to become visible

I look at the moon
like a little child
and I feel the moon is walking with me
to every place I go
It walks with me
step by step
I look at it and I smile
and I wave my hand
at it

I miss sitting with the moon without missiles

25TH MAY 2025

A Paper Plane

I wish I could be a paper plane for a few minutes
A paper plane that hugs the sky and freedom
A paper plane decorated with the colors of the beautiful Palestinian flag
A paper plane flying to any place I want
A paper plane drawing a smile on the face of the Gazan child

I wish I could be a paper plane for a few minutes
A paper plane flying in the sky with determination and strength
A paper plane hugging our loved ones that we lost in the sky
A paper plane that says I am here in my sky, I am more beautiful than your stupid planes
A paper plane with a strong soul made by Palestinian hands
A paper plane that has a sky and a beach and the winds and love and life

I wish I could be a paper plane for a few minutes
A paper plane that carries me to Jerusalem and Ramallah
A paper plane that takes me to the West Bank and its camps
A paper plane that demolishes the apartheid walls and makes me hug my loved ones in Nablus

A paper plane that gives me fresh air and hope

30ᵀᴴ May 2025

In Just One Minute

In just one minute—or sixty seconds, call it what you will—
you have to leave.
You have to flee.
You must carry your soul in your hands and walk quickly...
to survive.

In just one minute, everything before your eyes draws near,
only to become a memory.
Everything you see departs from you—forever.

Your memories: the dining table,
the masterpiece your grandmother gave you
for your academic excellence,
the gifts from joyful occasions.
You try to gather what you can.

In just one minute.

It's a real warning—a warning echoed
in the sound of destruction, of bombing.
You try to collect everything in the house you can carry.

I took what I could: my papers, my academic certificates,
my school books.
But I couldn't take it all.
It was too much.
My memories were beautiful—and too many.

My room overflowed with books, love, hope, memories, pictures,
pens,
the Quran,
my closet, my clothes,
the jar of olives, the vases, the lentils,
my birth certificate, my hair combs,
my white office sheets—the color of life,
my razor, my flash drive,
my virtual books, my passport photos,
my travel and university documents.

In one minute.

Alone—completely alone—you try to gather it all.
But memories?
How do you carry those?
Where do you put them?

They remain—etched in the house,
in the walls, in the people, in the photos,
in every corner, in every window.
Thousands of memories you must leave behind.
But how?

Why?

Why would I abandon the most beautiful parts of my life?
Because an unjust occupation wants to strip everything from me?

I jolted back to the moment.
There was still time.
I believe I had 13 seconds left—
13 seconds to carry everything with me,
and survive.

In just one minute,
I found the strength to endure.
To protect those around me—
with hope, with steadfastness.
We cried together, ran together, held one another—
until we reached zero.
The moment time ran out.

In just one minute,
the sound of planes arrived,
and the beautiful, innocent city began to shake.
From afar, I stood among thousands,
praying, begging for those wild moments to pass.

The bombs fell again—
followed by screams,
crying,
pain.

In just one minute,
I became addicted to playing the hero.
Time and again, I emerged unharmed—
as though I were Batman in some movie,
always surviving,
everything around me seemingly intact.

Until I began to breathe again, slowly.
I thought I'd survived.
I thought the monster had spared me.
More than 600 days passed in this nightmare of pain.

I thought I made it...
Until I saw the eyes of a child—
an innocent boy,
crying for his mother,
trying to wake her.
She had gone, forever, to heaven.

In that moment,
his tiny voice,
his grief—
defeated me.

This...
This is the minute in Gaza.
Now.

1ST JUNE 2025

Palestine Eid

On Eid... we cry in unseen silence.
On this Eid,
we light the lamps of memory on the thresholds of absence.
We rearrange the seats,
hoping the souls might return—
to fill the void with their shadows.

We remember those who have departed,
leaving behind only the echo of laughter
and the scent of perfume on sorrowful pillows.

We remember those whose doors Eid knocks upon,
only to find the wind.
Those with no home to embrace them,
nor a voice to call them by their warm name.

We remember those torn by war,
whose bodies lie bare in exile,
whose Eid songs were silenced,
whose garments of joy were lost in the throes of grief.

We remember the mothers,
waiting, for letters that never arrive,

for an embrace frozen in the memory of night.

We remember those locked in prison cells,
who see the sun only in dreams,
whose holidays are assassinated at cruel dawns
that knows no mercy.

For every orphaned heart,
waiting, for a reunion that never came,
for faces swallowed by absence...

For every mother surviving on hope,
walking the streets,
hearing nothing but silence.

But Eid is coming.
and Palestine will rise from the rubble—
free, as God and the prophets promised.
Free, with a dawn like no sunset before.

Your Eid is near, Palestine,
and I will be there—
to kiss your forehead,
to lay a carpet of hope upon your land.

Celebrate, Palestine, with your people.
Raise the banner of joy high.
We declare: PALESTINE IS FREE.

6TH JUNE 2025

Professor of the Art of Hope

Part One

In the heart of Gaza—where memories intertwine with the pain of the present—sorrow shapes the rhythm of daily life, weaving itself into the fabric of existence under the weight of war. The sound of shells tearing through the night is not merely noise; it is a haunting melody, echoing endlessly in our ears, striking the strings of our hearts, and drilling into the soul with bullets made of memory. Yet even as life teeters on the edge of tragic chaos, hope still blooms in the gardens of our souls.

It was eight in the morning. The balconies shimmered with the quiet resilience of hope, as my family and I sat together, sharing a simple breakfast of bread and olive oil. Just as we began to speak about our small farm, I felt as though I had been slapped by time. A distant explosion—its pulse ringing in my ears—froze the world around us. Crumbs flew through the air, and our faces hardened into expressions of fear.

My eyes roam the alleys of Gaza. I see children playing next to the shattered remains of rockets, spreading joy like wildflowers under a stormy sky.

How does childhood bloom amidst so much devastation?

They are masters of the art of hope—artists of innocence—painting smiles across their faces just as dawn colors the edges of night.

Even in the midst of destruction, belonging to Gaza is a path to enduring beauty.

Here, one hand struggles against life's cruelty, while the other reaches out in compassion.

Neighbors line up not only for bread, but for each other—sharing what little they have, along with their dreams.

At dawn, women gather to prepare breakfast for parts of the neighborhood. Men gather by the minarets to pray, surrounded by the scent of soil, trees, and steadfast pride.

But dreams carry a price. And these fragile dreams float above us in the sky of helplessness, whispering to every child whose future gleams like a distant star.

To hold onto hope demands courage beyond imagination.

A question lingers in our hearts:

Will we ever build a brighter tomorrow?

Or will hope remain an unfinished chapter in the book of our history?

I feel surrounded by beings of light—each carrying a dream tucked inside their pocket.

And every dream looks up toward a sky with no barriers.

Here, where crisis dances with hope, the people of Gaza understand:

they are not victims of history,

but the authors of a future that flickers like sunlight behind gray clouds.

And so, I continue my journey in this land, drawing lines of hope along the pathways of pain.

I remind myself:

even in hardship, life is worth living—with dignity.

Dawn is coming.

And I am here—

with a thousand stories,

and a thousand dreams.

Part Two

Gaza Between Pain and Hope.

At the edges of the sea that cradle the borders of pain, Gaza stands like an open wound on the world's map—unhealed, yet pulsating with life against all odds. A city that writes its chapters in blood and tears, singing its hymns from beneath the rubble, as if knowing that life only gives itself to those who truly deserve it. Gaza is not just a besieged city—it is a spirit of fire and patience, balancing precariously on the tightrope between death and life.

It is the little girl who opens her eyes each morning to the drone of airplanes and falls asleep to the prayers of her mother, hoping her father will return from the hospital—or from beneath the rubble—alive. It is the old woman who memorizes the names of martyrs as she recites verses of the Quran, weeping silently in a sorrow too profound for words, felt deeply in every corner of the heart. Amidst the pain, there is a miracle taking root. In Gaza, hope is planted in dry soil. From the stones, a flower grows.

From the darkness of night, the light of a candle emerges. From the ruins of schools, the first letters of life are rewritten.

There is hope in a child's laughter, in the paintings of an artist who drew his homeland from ashes, and in the poems of poets who write on the siege's walls that homeland is not just geography—but memory, and an undying question.

Gaza teaches the world lessons about the true meaning of dignity.

While battles rage over seats of power and authority elsewhere, Gaza fights to survive—to live and nothing more.

It is the compass of conscience when it is lost, and a test of humanity when it is forgotten.

Gaza, caught between pain and hope, tells a never-ending story.

Between a shell and a smile, between burying martyrs and planting trees, life is born from the womb of ashes.

And perhaps, whenever the world says Gaza is finished, it rises to say:

"I AM HERE. I AM STILL BEATING. I AM STILL RESISTING. AND IN MY HEART, THERE IS STILL ROOM FOR DREAMS."

3RD JULY 2025

YAHYA AL HAMARNA—a Palestinian refugee and political science student majoring in international relations and diplomacy—is a writer and artist who seeks to express human rights and justice issues through words and his pen.

He believes that "a journey of a thousand miles begins with a one step" and he is steadily moving towards a future that holds within it hope.

المقاومة
أعمق
أشكال
الحب

Resistance
is the deepest
form of love

www.ingramcontent.com/pod-product-compliance
Lightning Source LLC
Chambersburg PA
CBHW020342010526
44119CB00048B/571